Written and Illustrated
by
Leah Beck

*All proceeds will be prayerfully donated
to carry on God's work.*

Packaged by WinePress Publishing, PO Box 428, Enumclaw, WA 98022. The views expressed or implied in this work do not necessarily reflect those of WinePress Publishing. Ultimate design, content, and editorial accuracy of this work is the responsibility of the author.

ISBN 1-57921-308-1

This book is especially for:

_____

From:

_____

Date:_____

The Lord keeps watch over
you as you come and go,
both now and forevermore.
Psalms 121:8
(THE BOOK)

Acknowledgments

We would like to thank all of our friends, family and neighbors, who have encouraged us to share our story. Your kind words and heart-warming responses to My Grandma's Angels motivated us to continue our efforts in telling others about how God reached out and personally touched our lives.

We would also like to thank all of our teachers, pastors, youth leaders, Sunday School teachers, bible study friends, babysitters, and camp counselors who continue to inspire us to lead a Christian life and who have set such wonderful examples for us to follow. You have made an enormous difference in our lives. Thank you for giving your time and talents to the Lord and for sharing them with us!

We'd also like to thank those special friends who helped us share the home-made copies of My Grandma's Angels, as well as our dear friends who helped us during our publishing process with their various areas of expertise.

The publishing of this book would not have been possible without the love and support of Leah's dad and grandpa. We want to thank them from the bottom of our hearts!

We are very blessed by the angels (both earthly and heavenly) God has placed along our path to walk beside us while we are on this earth. Thank You, Jesus for sending your heavenly angels to comfort us with Your love.

Leah & Carol Beck

I'd like to dedicate this book to my
Papa and Mowie, who love me so much!
Thank you, God, for my family and friends.
Leah

1999

1994

A note from Leah's mom -

In early 1995, the Lord peacefully took my mother to heaven. God revealed to me His awesome plan and how much He loves us.

My mom and my dad adopted me when I was only four days old, and they were in their mid-forties. My parents are from farming families and my mom never lost her green thumb. She was a very kind and gentle-woman who enjoyed getting her hands in the dirt and watching God take over from there. She loved to plant bulbs in the fall and greatly antici-pated their ground-breaking entrance each spring.

During the last twenty years of her life, my mom battled strokes, heart attacks, and congestive heart failure. I remember many spine-chilling phone calls from my dad telling me it didn't look like she would make it this time. I'd drive an hour and a half to their small hospital in Southern Illi-nois, trying to focus on the road through my tears, wondering if she would still be alive by the time I made it to the emergency room.

The stress about my mom's health became so intense that I became physically ill. I worried about the time and the circumstances of her pass-ing and whether I would be able to spend those last precious moments with her. As God has shown me, my anxious feelings were futile. I didn't realize that God has this perfect plan for all of us.

My mom was nearing 80 years old when my husband and I finally told her she was going to be a grandma. She was very excited about being a grandma and her health greatly improved upon the arrival of those grandbabies. She and my dad loved being called Mowie and Papa.

Our second child, Leah, and my mom were very close. Leah enjoyed sitting calmly and playing with dolls with Mowie. Being the middle child between two very active brothers, Leah loved those special times when she played with Mowie all by herself.

On Valentine's weekend in 1995, we traveled to my hometown in Illinois. Our children felt excited about giving Papa and Mowie their homemade Valentine's gifts. On Sunday we went to brunch after church. After getting out of the car, my mom fell backward over a concrete wheel stopper. I saw her fall, but I wasn't close enough to help her. While I was watching her fall, I couldn't believe my eyes. She fell backward in such slow motion that she landed underneath the car unscathed. I asked her how on earth did she fall that slowly and gently. I'm sure now that it wasn't of the earth—but God's angels catching her and laying her down gently, especially after I saw this Bible verse.

> For He will command His angels concerning you to guard you in
> all your ways; they will lift you up in their hands, so that you will
> not strike your foot against a stone.
> Psalms 91:11-12 (NIV)

The next weekend Mowie and Papa came to our house. Our whole family was together, playing and enjoying each other's company for the entire weekend. At the time I didn't realize how much I'd appreciate that time spent with my dearest loved ones.

As it turned out, God allowed me to spend those last precious hours with my mom. Although we had anticipated my mom's death for many years, we certainly didn't expect it that weekend. Mowie's passing couldn't have been more serene as she died on Sunday night in her sleep. And through my daughter's beautiful dream, God sent me a peace that surpasses understanding.

Leah's story tells the rest of the events as they happened.

Mowie and Papa came to our house a lot. Sometimes we went to play at their house in Sparta.

My Mowie was a special
grandma. She loved me very
much. She was a great hugger.

Mowie played Barbies and
dolls with me. I think she had
as much fun as I did!

One weekend in February 1995, Mowie and Papa came for the weekend. On Saturday, we went to Michael's basketball game and Boy Scout supper. Mowie and I laughed at the funny   magician.

On Sunday, Mowie watched me dance with my ballet and tap shoes. She also played Barbies and Polly Pockets with me.

On Sunday night Mowie, Michael, Mom and I snuggled on the couch under a blanket and watched the movie about a baby bear whose mother died.

I hugged and kissed Mowie

and Papa good night and

we all went to bed.

During the night, the angels came to me in my dream. The angels were holding Mowie's hand and they told me they were taking her to heaven. The angels were smiling and were very nice. I wasn't afraid of the angels.

I knew
they were taking
Mowie to a
wonderful place.

The next morning when I woke up, everyone especially my mom and Papa were very sad. I sat on my mom's lap and she told me that Mowie went to heaven during the night. I told her that I already knew because the angels had told me in my dream.

My mom seemed surprised that I already knew about Mowie. She asked me a lot of questions about my special dream. I think it made her happy to hear about Mowie going to heaven. I told my mommy all about how beautiful and happy they all were.

The angels were wearing pretty white dresses. They had golden halos and wings. The angels were much bigger than Mowie. They had beautiful long curly yellow hair.

Mowie gave me a kiss and then I felt they all loved me a lot. Then the angels took Mowie to heaven to see Jesus.

One night a couple of months later, my mommy and daddy went to an auction at Michael's school. The next morning mommy showed me a picture they bought at the auction.

It looked exactly like
my dream about Mowie going to
heaven! It was beautiful.

Mommy asked me what the
picture made me think of.
I said "Mowie."

A teacher at Michael's school, Sister Busch made the picture of my dream with a needle and different colors of thread. I don't know how she knew about my dream of Mowie and the angels. Everything in the picture was just like my dream. It took Sister Busch over a year to make the picture.

My mom said she prayed that I wouldn't forget my Mowie or my special dream. I think God asked Sister Busch to make that beautiful picture for me so I will never forget my dream or God's promise of living in heaven with him.

I know someday
we'll all be
together again.

I miss my Mowie. She was a great hugger and snuggler. I know she is very happy there. I got to see the angels taking her to heaven, that was very special. 🙂

In all things God works for the good of those who love Him, who have been called according to His purpose.

Romans 8:28 (NIV)

More from Leah's mom -

Leah was only four and a half when the angels visited her in a dream and took Mowie to heaven! As I reflect on this, I try to understand why the angels appeared to Leah. In Matthew 11:25, Jesus said, *"I praise you, Father, Lord of heaven and earth, because you have hidden these things from the wise and learned, and revealed them to little children"* (NIV). A child's sweet innocence, honesty, and strong faith are an undeniable witness to God's awesome plan and His powerful love.

The angel's visit was a blessing from God that helped ease our painful loss. Leah was never upset—she knew exactly where Mowie had gone—and she knew it was a place full of love and peace. Leah's faith and belief in Jesus is so strong! By watching my children and their faith, I realize the importance of that childlike faith which Jesus emphasized in His teachings. Children are truly gifts from God with their wide-eyed wonder and their hearts full of the pureness of God's love. Jesus said, *"Let the little children come to me, and do not hinder them, for the kingdom of God belongs to such as these"* Matthew 19:13–15, Mark 10:13–16, and Luke 18:15–17 (NIV).

When my mom died, I was very upset, but at the same time I had this overwhelming calmness. *"Blessed are those who mourn, for they will be comforted"* Matthew 5:4 (NIV). We were all stunned by what Leah was telling us that morning. I wanted to know every single detail about her dream, the angels, and Mowie going to heaven. I was amazed that Leah slept the entire night especially with all the people coming and going. Truly amazing things can happen in the presence of angels. Our sons were awakened right away by all of the commotion. Leah rarely slept through the night, even when the house was perfectly quiet! This is just another example that nothing is impossible for God. *". . . with God, all things are possible"* Matthew 19:26 and Mark 10:27 (NIV).

My mom was never very vocal about her faith. The way she led her life and a few precious thoughts she left behind help me know that she trusted God with her life and the plan He had for her. I recently noticed a plaque still hanging in Papa and Mowie's house that displays a very simple little poem, but it really says it all!

> In my hand, I hold today.
> In my dreams, I hold tomorrow.
> In my faith, I hold forever.
> author unknown

Living forever in heaven is an awesome opportunity from God, and Mowie knew that was where she would go when she left this earth.

Because of God's greatest gift, I don't have to worry about my mom anymore - her eyesight is restored, she won't fall down and break any more bones, and no more trips by ambulance. Her biggest worry of being unable to take care of herself is no longer a concern because Mowie is now in the loving arms of Jesus. *"For God so loved the world that He gave His one and only Son, that whoever believes in Him shall not perish but have eternal life"* John 3:16 (NIV).

The coincidence of Sister Busch's beautiful counted cross-stitch resembling Leah's dream sent tears streaming down my face. Our second little "miracle" also helps me understand my view of life compared with God's vision. My impression is similar to the backside of a counted cross-stitch. Many knots and colorful threads are going in every direction seemingly without meaning or purpose. As I struggle through my life day by day (stitch by stitch), I now realize those unpleasant experiences (knots) are opportunities to grow (change colors), strengthen my faith and trust God to finish the work he has begun in me. *"Being confident of this very thing, that He who has begun a good work in you will complete it until the day of Jesus Christ"* Philippians 1:6 (NKJV). From God's view (the front of the cross-stitch), every single tiny stitch has a purpose and they harmonize together perfectly to create a finely crafted work of art. *"God has made everything beautiful in its time. He has also set eternity in the hearts of men; yet they cannot fathom what God has done from beginning to end"* Ecclesiastes 3:11 (NIV).

Every time I think about how everything fell perfectly into place, I thank God for His wonderful gift and His perfect plan for my mother and for each one of us. *"There is a time and a season for every purpose under heaven: a time to be born and a time to die, . . . a time to weep and a time to laugh, a time to mourn and a time to dance . . ."* Ecclesiastes 3:1–2 (THE LIVING BIBLE).

The plan God has for us is more amazing than we could ever begin to imagine for ourselves if we follow God's will instead of our own. God knows our every thought and every action. He understands us better than we understand ourselves. *"You created my inmost being, you knit me together in my mother's womb"* Psalms 139:13 (NIV).

It's amazing to me how God concerns Himself with every little detail. *"For your Father knows what you need before you ask him"* Matthew 6:8 (NIV). Our God, who created heaven and earth, loves us enough to know everything about us! Jesus said, *"And even the very hairs of your head are all numbered"* Matthew 10:30 (NIV).

I am thankful to God for so many things. I know that everything we have on this earth is a gift from God. Through all of this, I have learned just how applicable the words of the Bible are in our everyday lives. The Bible is the best guide to how we should live our lives with the best role model for us and for our children - Jesus Christ!

These days, I worry less than I did before this all happened. Unfortunately I still worry a little (I think it's a mom thing), but now I always pray when I'm worried. I trust God and His perfect plan for us. *"Don't worry about anything; instead pray about everything. Tell God your needs and don't forget to thank Him for His answers. If you do this you will experience God's peace, which is far more wonderful than the human mind can understand. His peace will keep your thoughts and your hearts quiet and at rest as you trust in Christ Jesus"* Philippians 4:6–7 (NIV).

Since my mother died, I have drawn closer to God. I know the strong faith and peace I feel are wonderful treasures that are mine only because of God's grace. Many times I have heard "GRACE" explained as an acronym—God's Riches At Christ's Expense. *"Because of his kindness, you*

*have been saved through trusting Christ. And even trusting is not of your-
selves; it too is a gift from God. Salvation is not a reward for the good we
have done, so none of us can take any credit for it. It is God Himself who has
made us what we are and given us new lives from Christ Jesus; and long
ages ago He planned that we should spend these lives in helping others"*
Ephesians 2:8–9 (THE LIVING BIBLE).

When I allowed God's love to fill that empty lonely void in my heart,
my whole attitude about my mom's death changed. Now when I think
about her, I rejoice because I know she lives in that special place in heaven
that Jesus prepared for her. Jesus said, *"There are many rooms in my Father's
home, and I am going to prepare a place for you. If this were not so, I would
tell you plainly. When everything is ready, I will come and get you, so that you
will always be with me where I am"* John 14:2–3 (THE BOOK). The peace I
enjoy is a great comfort because I know that someday I'll join her! That
assurance could only come from my faith in Jesus!

We wanted to put this true story into words and pictures in hopes that
others would be comforted. God has a wonderful plan for each one of us
and that plan includes heaven! *"For I know the plans I have for you,"* de-
clares the Lord, *"plans to prosper you and not to harm you, plans to give you
hope and a future"* Jeremiah 29:11 (NIV).

God's help is all I need to get through any difficulties in my life. By
praying and trusting in Jesus, I have tranquility in even the most other-
wise unbearable circumstances, as well as in life's daily demands. Jesus
said, *"Come to me all who are weary and burdened, and I will give you rest"*
Matthew 11:28 (NIV).

Thank you, God, for my dear family, for your awesome peace, for your
perfect plan and especially for the wonderful gift of your Son, Jesus Christ!

> *May the Lord bless and protect you;*
> *May the Lord's face radiate*
> *with joy because of you;*
> *May He be gracious to you,*
> *Show you His favor*
> *and give you His peace.*
> Numbers 6:24–27 (THE LIVING BIBLE)

Their life will be like a watered garden,
and all their sorrows will be gone,"
says the Lord . . .
"I will turn their mourning into joy.
I will comfort them and exchange
their sorrow for rejoicing."
Jeremiah 31:12-13 (THE BOOK)

My Grandma's favorite
Bible verse or saying:

Me and My Grandma

Me and My Grandpa

My Grandpa's favorite
Bible verse or saying:

To order additional copies of

My
Grandma's
Angels

Call (877) 421-READ (7323)

or send $12.00 each + $3.95* S&H to

WinePress Publishing
P.O. Box 428
Enumclaw, WA 98022

* add $1.00 for each additional book ordered

Order directly from the author:

My Grandma's Angels
PO Box 193
Cottleville, MO 63338-0193

website: www.mygrandmasangels.com
email: mygrandmasangels1@juno.com

It is our prayer that many people will be helped and comforted by God's personal touch in *My Grandma's Angels*. If you would like to write to us, please use the author's addresses above.